Spilling the Beans...

Marie Antoinette

First published in 2000 by Miles Kelly Publishing,
Bardfield Centre, Great Bardfield, Essex CM7 4SL

Printed in Italy

ISBN 1-902947-62-2

24681097531

Cover design and illustration: Inc
Layout design: GQ
Art Direction: Clare Sleven

Spilling the Beans on...
Marie Antoinette

by **Mick Gowar**

Illustrations   Mike Mosedale

About the Author

Mick Gowar has written or edited over 40 books for children, including collections of poetry, novels, graphic novels, picture books and short stories. He has visited over 600 schools, libraries, colleges, and other venues to give talks and performances of his work, or to lead workshops. As well as writing and performing, he is at present a part-time lecturer in the Department of Illustration and Graphic Arts at Anglia University, Cambridge.

Contents

Introduction

Let Them Eat Cake?

Spilling the beans usually means revealing shocking and surprising facts about someone, something they wouldn't like other people to know – like a criminal record or unpleasant personal habits.

In the case of Marie Antoinette, the facts I want to reveal may be surprising, but they may make you think she was a nicer person than you thought she was.

Many people believe that when Marie Antoinette heard that the poor people of Paris were starving because they had no bread to eat, she cruelly said: "Then let them eat cake."

This *was* said by a queen of France, but it was said almost 100 years earlier by a wife of Louis *XIV*, not by Marie Antoinette who was the wife of Louis *XVI*. But Marie Antoinette's enemies claimed that it was she who had said it. It was one of the many lies and rumours that were spread about Marie Antoinette by her numerous enemies.

She had enemies at her husband's court and enemies among the many people who wanted to change the way France was ruled. These enemies created an image of Marie Antoinette as someone who was cruel, uncaring and vicious. When the Revolution came, the image was taken as true and Marie Antoinette paid with her life for the rumours and lies which other people spread about her.

She had her faults. She was careless with money and gave expensive gifts and well-paid jobs to her friends and favourites.

But you may be surprised to discover that she wasn't the cruel, heartless monster many people think she was, when I *Spill the Beans* about Marie Antoinette.

Chapter 1

Playing Mums and Dads

Marie Antoinette was born in the Hofberg Palace in Vienna, the capital of the Austrian Empire, on 2nd November, 1755. Her mother was the Empress of Austria, Maria Theresa.

Maria Theresa wasn't just the wife of a king (or in this case, emperor). Like the present Queen of England she was the ruler; the woman in charge.

Marie Antoinette's father Francis had been the Duke of Lorraine. He also had the title *Holy Roman Emperor*, but in reality he didn't have any power. He was just the husband of the monarch, a sort of 18th century Duke of Edinburgh.

But being the husband of the empress wasn't really a full-time job. Francis had tried a few jobs, but he either didn't like them or wasn't very good at them.

He'd tried the army, but he was no good as a general and the empress's husband couldn't be given a lower rank.

He wasn't any good at helping with all the paperwork to do with running the Empire, because his reading and writing were so poor, especially his spelling (today he'd probably be called dyslexic).

He was good at maths, though, and helped organize the royal finances. But the thing Francis liked best was hunting stags in the woods around Vienna. When it came to running the Austrian Empire he left that to his wife, Maria Theresa.

His only real job was to help Maria Theresa make lots of little princes and princesses. He was very good at that. He and Maria Theresa had 16 children. They had so many because in the mid-18th century most children didn't live to be more than four or five years old, even the children of kings and emperors. Children died in their thousands from smallpox, TB and measles. The first inoculations against these diseases weren't developed until the end of the century.

Today we'd probably call Maria Theresa a workaholic. She never stopped working, even to have babies.

On the day that Marie Antoinette was born, Maria Theresa refused to go bed. She sat in a low armchair, still reading and signing important state papers. When the labour pains got too strong, she put down her pen and gave birth in the chair. Then she checked to see if her eleventh child was alright, handed the baby over to the nurse, picked up her pen and went back to work.

Nanny knows best... but Mother knows better

Like most royal children, Marie Antoinette – along with her brothers and sisters – was brought up by nannies and private tutors. But these private tutors were the best that Maria Theresa could get and nobody *ever* said "No" to Maria Theresa.

Marie Antoinette's Italian teacher was the famous playwright Metastasio, and the even more famous composer Gluck taught her to play the spinet and clavichord (these were early keyboard instruments; the piano hadn't been invented

yet). Gluck and Metastasio may not be very well known now, but they were in their day. It was the equivalent of Prince Charles paying David Beckham to be Prince Harry's personal football coach, or persuading Elton John to give him weekly piano lessons.

The royal children all had music lessons and they formed a band to give musical performances to entertain their parents. Marie Antoinette's eldest brother, Joseph, played the cello, her sister Christina played the clavichord, Marie Antoinette sang and her brother Ferdinand played the timpani.

You would probably assume that being royal children they would be spoilt; given all the toys they wanted and served their favourite food for every meal. Not a bit of it. Maria Theresa was a very strict mother. She wanted her children to be polite and obedient. This is part of a letter she wrote to the royal nanny about the children's food:

I insist on their eating everything, with no fault finding and no picking and choosing. Further, they must not be allowed to criticize their food.

On Fridays, Saturdays and all other fast days they will eat fish… All my children seem to have an aversion to fish, but they must all overcome this, there is to be no relenting in this matter.

See that they eat sugar as little as possible.

Future husband and future king

Meanwhile, in the palace of Versailles, the boy who would grow up to be Marie Antoinette's husband and the future King Louis XVI of France was being brought up the Versailles way – *according to the rules.*

Versailles was the vast palace which Louis's great-great-grandfather, King Louis XIV, had built just outside Paris near the village of Versailles. It was vast, and it was the most luxurious palace in the whole of Europe. It was also the stuffiest and most formal.

Hundreds of lords, ladies and nobles lived at Versailles as courtiers. They spent all their time trying to be the king's or queen's favourite by giving them expensive presents or by saying flattering things to them. They hoped that if they were a royal favourite they might get important and powerful jobs, which also meant lots and lots of money. As you can imagine, all the lords and ladies and nobles were always gossiping about each other, spreading rumours to get their rivals into trouble and out of favour.

To keep this army of jealous and quarrelsome nobles in order, the palace was run on strict lines of precedence: that means that everyone in Versailles had a place they had to keep to, and everything that happened in the palace had strict rules. For example, if the king was to go for a walk in the gardens of his palace, there were rules to say who was allowed to walk beside him, who was allowed to walk immediately behind him, who was allowed to walk next, and next, and next and so on.

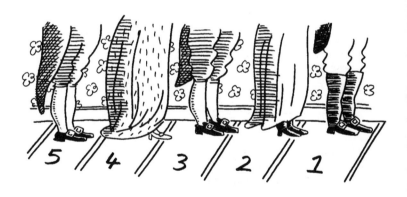

This was even true of bringing up babies. Like most babies of wealthy parents, Louis had a wet nurse (a woman who was employed to breastfeed him) and other people to look after him. But there were strict rules on who could do what. One of Louis's aunts wrote:

The wet nurse's only function is to suckle the child when he is brought to her; she may not touch him. There are cradle-rockers and other ladies whose job that is, but they may not take orders from the wet nurse. There are set hours for giving the child exercise, three or four times a day. When the hour strikes, even if the child is sleeping, he is woken up for exercise.

When Louis was older he started lessons in the palace. He spent seven hours a day in school work. He learnt Latin and three sorts of history: biblical, classical and French. (History was Louis's best subject.) He also learnt geography, physics, religion, political theory and mathematics.

Here's one of the maths problems that Louis was given when he was 11 years old. See if you can do it.

On 10th February 1766, three princes have a combined age of 30 years and 11 days; the second is one year, two months and 24 days younger than the first; and the third is one year, 10 months and 22 days younger than the second. Calculate the age of each of the princes.

Answers

Prince No. 1: 11 years, five months and 18 days

Prince No. 2: 10 years, two months and 23 days

Prince No. 3: Eight years, four months and one day

It's a very difficult sum unless you happened to be in the royal family. It was a sum specially made up to make maths more interesting to the royal children. The answer is the exact ages of Louis and his two brothers, the Duke of Provence and the Duke of Artois, on 10th February 1766.

The boy who was born to be king

Louis wasn't very good at his lessons, but he wasn't stupid. If he'd gone to a school he would probably have been somewhere near the middle of the class in tests and exams.

But that didn't worry his grandfather the king, or his father the dauphin (that was the French title for the heir to the throne, like in Britain the heir to the throne has the title Prince of Wales). They didn't mind that Louis wasn't terrifically bright because Louis was never going to be king (or so they thought).

Louis had an older brother, the Duke of Bourgogne, who would one day – everybody agreed – be one of the best kings of France ever. He was a brilliant child, so clever that his teachers had to work hard to keep up with him.

Then in 1760, when Louis was six years old, his brother Bourgogne became very ill. He had a disease called *tuberculosis* (which is also called TB). Usually TB infects the lungs, but the type of TB Bourgogne caught infected his bones, making it impossible for him to walk or move without pain. Soon Bourgogne had to stop lessons and spend all day either in bed or a wheelchair. Nowadays, TB would be treated with powerful drugs called antibiotics, but these drugs hadn't been discovered in the 18th century. There was nothing anyone, including the doctors, could do except wait and hope the little prince would get better.

Louis was moved out of the nursery so that he could spend time cheering up his sick older brother. The two boys played cards or with toy soldiers until poor Bourgogne got too tired. Gradually Bourgogne got paler and thinner, but the royal doctors couldn't do anything for him. On Easter Saturday 1761 the brilliant little prince died.

Now that Bourgogne was dead, Louis was second in line to the throne of France. If he survived – and more than half of all children at the time died in childhood – he was certain to be King of France. Louis's life would never be the same again.

But Bourgogne's death wouldn't just change Louis's life completely, it would change Marie Antoinette's life, too.

Chapter 2

Engaged To a Boy She'd Never Met

Never in the 900 years of the French monarchy had there been an Austrian-born queen of France. It was unthinkable. For as long as there had been a France and an Austria the two countries had been the bitterest of enemies.

Ever since the collapse of the Roman Empire, in around AD476, France and Austria had been rivals; competing to see who could be the strongest, most powerful country in Europe.

The pattern had been the same for centuries: whenever a country declared war on Austria, France would help Austria's

The French Look like their Food...

enemy; and whenever a country declared war on France, Austria would take the side of France's enemy. Almost from birth little French boys and girls were brought up to hate little Austrian boys and girls, and vice versa.

For centuries, France and Austria had fought each other to be top nation, but in the early 18th century a new rival to both countries emerged. The German state of Prussia, on the south coast of the Baltic Sea, had become more and more powerful and wanted to control Europe. In 1756, when Marie Antoinette and Louis were still babies, a great war started – the *Seven Years' War*. Austria and France were, for the first time in history, on the same side against Prussia and its main ally, Britain.

The war was a disaster for France. It lasted seven years, cost a fortune and France lost – badly. As part of the peace treaty, France was forced to give most of its American colonies and parts of India to Britain. Worst of all, Prussia was now a major power.

Despite the two countries' long history of past quarrels and wars, France and Austria were determined to stay allies. It was the only way they could protect themselves against the mighty Prussian army. The King of France and the Empress of Austria agreed on a way to show what good friends they now were. It was the traditional way in which countries had always done it: with a royal wedding.

After years of bargaining a deal was finally agreed: the King of France's grandson, Louis, would marry the Empress of Austria's daughter, Marie Antoinette. At the time of the engagement, Louis was 14 years old and Marie Antoinette was just 13. They had never met.

How to be Queen of France

Marie Antoinette's education changed as soon as the engagement was agreed. The French Foreign Minister sent a French tutor to teach Marie Antoinette all about France. He was a librarian and priest called Vermond.

During his first few days in Vienna Vermond tested her to see how much she knew. He reported back to his bosses in the French government.

Marie Antoinette: TEST RESULTS

Very poor. Her education has obviously been neglected. She was unable to identify *any* of the regiments of the French army from the colour of the uniforms. Also, she did not know the names of any of the colonels of the French army.

Grade: F – *Must do better when she is married.*

Poor Marie Antoinette.

The French government also sent a dentist from Paris to look after her teeth and a hairdresser to arrange her hair in the latest French fashion (this was very difficult, because Marie Antoinette had reddish hair which was extremely frizzy).

Marie Antoinette's mother also helped train her daughter to be a queen by taking her to operas, ballets and balls and teaching her to gamble at the palace casino. Maria Theresa's advice to her daughter was short and not terribly sweet:

How to be a successful Queen of France

1. Make the French people love you

2. Stay out of politics

3. Always look gentle and fluffy

4. Don't offend anyone

5. Do as your husband tells you

It wasn't the sort of advice that Maria Theresa herself had ever followed, but it was quite good advice, because that's how the French nobility and the French people expected queens to behave. Unfortunately for her, Marie Antoinette didn't manage to follow her mother's advice.

Stripped!

On 21st April 1770, Marie Antoinette left Vienna for her
wedding. She was followed by a magnificent procession of
48 coaches, but she was very unhappy. She was leaving her
mother and her family behind. None of them was coming to
the wedding, and Marie Antoinette didn't know when she
would see any of them again.

Travelling without her family was all part of the agreement
between France and Austria. As the wife of the future
King of France, Marie Antoinette was to leave everything of
her past life behind; she was to stop being Austrian and
become French.

To show the world that Marie Antoinette had changed into a
French princess, a bizarre ceremony was organised on a tiny
island in the middle of the River Rhine on the border with
France, near the town of Strasbourg.

French carpenters built a wooden pavilion on the island. It
was a very odd building, half way between a miniature palace
and a beach hut. There were two main rooms, one facing the
Austrian (and German) side of the river, one facing the French
side. Marie Antoinette entered by the 'Austrian' door with her

Austrian ladies-in-waiting, who had travelled with her from Vienna. The Austrian ladies-in-waiting took off all her clothes and pushed her through a doorway into the 'French' side where French ladies-in-waiting dressed her in a complete new set of French clothes.

Not surprisingly, being stripped naked in front of complete strangers proved too much for the 14-year-old Marie Antoinette and she burst into tears.

Almost as upsetting were the decorations on the 'French' side. The walls were covered with tapestries showing one of the most tragic marriages in Greek mythology. On one side of the room was the hero Jason, with his dead children at his feet, watching the murderer escape in a carriage pulled by dragons. On the other side was a tapestry showing Jason's wife dying in the most appalling agony.

The German poet and playwright Goethe went with a group of friends to look at the pictures before the ceremony took place and was horrified by what he saw.

"What!" I exclaimed to my companions. "Will they show this to the young queen at the very first step she makes into her new country, the picture of the most horrible of marriages?" ...Had they nothing more appropriate than these frightful spectres to show to their beautiful queen on her first arrival?

A week later, Marie Antoinette met her husband, Louis, the dauphin, for the first time. Two days later they were married in the chapel of the palace of Versailles, her new home.

Chapter 3

Rules, Rules and More Rules

Marie Antoinette had been born and brought up in a palace, but she still found it very difficult to get used to living in Versailles.

Compared to Versailles, her mother's palace had been quite easy going. Neither her mother nor her father had been keen on long ceremonial dinners or elaborate court rituals. But in Versailles everything was run by customs, ceremonies and rules.

There were rules for everything, and Marie Antoinette hated them. For example, getting dressed in the morning. At the Hofberg, where she'd grown up, Marie Antoinette had been helped to dress in the morning by servants. It was no big deal. In Versailles, dressing the dauphine (that means the wife of the dauphin) was a huge ceremony involving up to a dozen duchesses, countesses and ladies-in-waiting.

Only the most senior lady at court was allowed to hand a dauphine or a queen her underclothes or pick out her hair ribbons. Marie Antoinette often had to wait ages, stark naked in an unheated room, for a lady of the proper rank to arrive so that she could be handed her stockings. Every morning she had to watch while a line of noblewomen passed her petticoat

from one to the other, in strict order of rank, like a bucket chain. Understandably, she would often yawn with boredom, or make jokes to pass the time while she waited for some piece of clothing to be passed to the most senior duchess or princess so they could pass it to her.

Marie Antoinette's lack of 'respect' for their rules horrified the French nobility. Rules were their life. Without the rules of court life at Versailles it would be impossible to see who was superior to whom. In fact, without the elaborate rules of behaviour, many of the nobles at Versailles would have no job and no purpose.

The French lords and ladies started to spread sly rumours about Marie Antoinette's lack of respect for customs and rules. She wasn't a good choice of dauphine, the gossipers said, and she'd make a terrible queen. It was a stupid idea to have a French dauphin marry an Austrian, they whispered, and it would all end in disaster.

Candle in the window

Nowadays vaccination against smallpox is so common that the disease has been almost wiped out in Europe. Until the end of the 18th century, however, there was no vaccination and no real treatment. It was a common disease and many people, like Marie Antoinette herself, were disfigured by the scars from the spots. But it wasn't just an infectious childhood disease like chicken pox; many people died of smallpox.

In April 1774 King Louis XV became ill. The king's doctors treated him in the way they treated most of their patients' diseases, by bleeding.

Doctors in those days believed that many diseases could be cured by removing blood from their patients. Sometimes they put bloodsucking worms called leeches on the patient's arms or legs to suck the blood out, or they simply cut open a vein with a scalpel and bound up the wound when they thought they'd taken enough blood.

Twice they bled the king, but it didn't do any good. The king had caught smallpox.

Neither Louis nor Marie Antoinette were allowed to see the old king in case they caught the disease. As the king got worse a lighted candle was placed in his bedroom window. When the candle was blown out that would be the sign that the king was dead.

Anxiously, Louis and Marie Antoinette watched the king's bedroom window from their own rooms. Just after 3 o'clock on the morning of 10th April the candle was blown out. Louis was now King Louis XVI and Marie Antoinette was Queen.

King and Queen

The new king and queen must have looked like an ill-matched couple. She was small and delicate. Her favourite amusements were going to the theatre and opera with her friends, or having informal parties.

The king was a big man, muscular and full of energy. His favourite hobby was hunting – riding powerful horses cross-country all day long, chasing deer or wild boar.

Louis also really enjoyed hard, physical work like digging ditches and bricklaying. When he was younger, he'd learnt to plough, and the first picture Marie Antoinette ever saw of her future husband was a drawing of him ploughing a field.

The Austrian ambassador (and Maria Theresa's personal spy)
Count Mercy wrote to the empress:

> He has an extraordinary taste for everything in the way of building, masonry, carpentry and other things of this kind. He is always having something rearranged in his apartments and he himself works with the workmen, moving materials, beams and paving stones, giving himself up for hours at a time to this strenuous exercise.

Louis was also much happier talking to the workmen who came to build the fences or clear the drains than to the grand courtiers of Versailles. Like many of his family, Louis was very shy. He'd also been brought up with a rather poor opinion of himself. He was never a favourite child. He knew that his parents always thought Bourgogne was much cleverer than he was and would have made a better dauphin and king. When Bourgogne died, his younger brother the Count of Provence became his parents' favourite. Louis was brought up to think of himself as others thought of him: second best.

The one thing Louis seems to have been really talented at was making locks. He had a workshop with a small forge built at the palace. He would spend hours in his workshop, making and repairing locks.

Chapter 4

Victims of Fashion

In Europe in the 1770s the fashion for rich women was to wear incredibly uncomfortable and elaborate clothes and hairstyles. Every morning, noblewomen would be strapped into tight whalebone corsets, then climb into petticoats with huge hoops sewn into them, and then be encased in dresses encrusted with jewels and decorated with gold and silver thread. These dresses also had enormous padded hips sewn into them, called *paniers* (after the baskets which pack horses carried strapped to their sides).

These dresses were so heavy that it was impossible to move quickly when wearing them. The paniers were so wide it was

difficult getting through doors, and sometimes the corsets underneath were laced so tightly that it was difficult to breathe. It was no wonder that so many noblewomen in the 18th century had a reputation for fainting. It wasn't because they were so sensitive or delicate; it was because of the clothes they had to wear.

Big hair

The hairstyles were even more ridiculous than the dresses. The fashion in the late 1770s was for hairstyles to be worn as high as possible. The taller your hairstyle, the more important you were. Rich women's hairstyles were sometimes over a metre high and decorated with feathers, fabrics and jewels. One courtier at Versailles, the Duchess of Chartres, had a hairstyle made that included a scale model of her young son's nursery, complete with a little toy nanny, another servant and a parrot – her son's favourite pet.

When ladies had to travel by coach to balls or the theatre, they had to ride with their heads poking out of the window because there was no room inside for their enormous hair.

Like many of the other rules and customs in Versailles, Marie Antoinette hated the artificial clothes and hairstyles. She tried to change the fashion by wearing simple, straight dresses of white muslin, and wearing her hair down in what she called a 'natural' style.

She had her portrait painted several times by Elisabeth Vigée-Lebrun, who agreed with the Queen's ideas about fashion. These paintings show the Queen dressed in her simple, 'natural' clothes, often surrounded by her children or pets. Marie Antoinette also persuaded her friends like Princess la Lamballe and Gabrielle de Yolande Polignac to be painted in a similar way.

Once again our Austrian queen is showing no respect at all for our French rules and customs. Every time she comes across a rule, she breaks it. How can someone with so little respect for the ways of others, expect others to respect her?

Have you seen the recent portrait of our beloved queen painted by Mme Vigée-Lebrun? The queen is dressed, as she so often is these days, in a plain thin cotton dress that would look dowdy on a milk-maid.

Is this how a queen should dress? When our French garment industry is in such trouble, it should be the duty of the *Queen of France* to be seen wearing the finest *French* clothes. But no, not our little Austrian madame. Not content with treating our

But the 'natural' fashion never took off in Versailles. The ladies of the court hated the new look. Their elaborate dresses and hairstyles were two of the most important ways they could compete with each other. If everybody dressed plainly, they said, it would be impossible to see who was richer than who.

The vicious gossip and rumours against Marie Antoinette started again, worse than ever. The most jealous courtiers published anonymous pamphlets, almost poison pen letters, full of spiteful and sly attacks on Marie Antoinette.

customs with contempt, she also wants to ruin our fine *French* businesses by setting a fashion for wearing *cheap foreign-made clothes*.

Look at the picture closely when you have the chance. The fabric of the dress is so thin it's indecent. And we all know what women who wear clothes like that get up to…

We say:

WATCH YOUR WIFE, YOUR MAJESTY!

WE DON'T TRUST HER, AND WE DON'T THINK YOU SHOULD EITHER!

Once again, what the scandal-mongers hated was that Marie Antoinette was refusing to behave in the way they expected a queen to behave. That was:

 To smile a lot and not have any opinions on anything.

 To do as she was told by her husband and her advisers and courtiers.

 To have lots of babies – especially boys.

...And, so far, Marie Antoinette had shown no sign of doing any of them.

The theatre at the Petit Trianon

In the grounds of the palace of Versailles were two country houses: the Grand Trianon and the Petit Trianon. As a coronation present, Louis gave Marie Antoinette the Petit Trianon as her own private house and hideaway.

This was exactly what Marie Antoinette wanted most: the opportunity to be herself, not just to act the role of queen in the way that everyone expected her to.

At the Petit Trianon, Marie Antoinette tried to create her own little world. She had a little village of 12 cottages and a farm built in the grounds. She also had a theatre built so that she and some of her friends could act in the latest plays. Her company of actors included Marie Antoinette herself, her great friends Gabrielle Yolande de Polignac and Count Vaudreuil, and Louis's younger brother the Count of Artois.

A typical production, in August 1780, was a play called *The Village Prophet*. The cast were a village girl and boy called

Collette and Colin, who were played by the queen and the Count of Artois, and the prophet, who was played by Count Vaudreuil. The audience consisted of the king, the Count and Countess of Provence (the king's other brother and sister-in-law), the wife of Artois and the king's sister, Elisabeth.

YAWN !!!!

No grand courtiers or ministers at all were invited. They never *were* invited to Marie Antoinette's private plays. "I have no court here," Marie Antoinette said. "I live as a private individual."

It's what many kings and queens, princes and princesses have wished for throughout history, but it's something they can never have. There will always be courtiers, ministers or ordinary members of the public who won't allow it. They will always demand that a queen must behave like a queen – or rather *their* idea of how a queen should behave. And acting the part of a village maiden in a sentimental play *isn't* what they mean.

Chapter 5

The Queen's Favourites

Unfortunately, the queen and her little group of friends didn't just stick to acting and playing at farming. Marie Antoinette, whatever she might have claimed, still behaved like a queen in the way she rewarded her friends. She gave them and their families expensive gifts and jobs with big salaries in return for no real work.

One of her favourites was the Princess la Lamballe, who was famous for fainting when she got upset or excited. The princess was made *Superintendent of the Queen's Household*, which put her in charge of providing entertainments for the queen and rewarded her with an enormous salary.

PRINCESS LA LAMBALLE

Job title: Superintendent of the Queen's Household.

Qualifications: The queen liked her. Tended to faint when upset.

Salary: 150,000 livres* every year.

Duties: Organizing entertainments and amusements for the queen – like parties, dances, and theatre trips.

*Livre – French coin, worth about £2.50

Other favourites Marie Antoinette gave jobs and money to were Gabrielle Yolande de Polignac and Count Vaudreuil, who were both members of her little acting company.

GABRIELLE YOLANDE DE POLIGNAC

Job title: Governess to the Royal Children.

Qualifications: The queen liked her.

When she first came to court, the queen liked her so much that she gave Gabrielle de Polignac's husband a job at Versailles paying 12,000 livres. But being the queen's friend was an expensive business and the Polignacs soon got into debt. Marie-Antoinette then gave them 400,000 livres to pay off their debts and a whopping 800,000 livres towards a dowry for their daughter.

Duties: Organising the schooling of the royal children (but she didn't actually have to teach them anything).

And Gabrielle Yolande de Polignac also shared in the good fortune of her lover...

COUNT VAUDREUIL

OUCH!

Job titles: Grand Falconer of France, Governor of Lille, Marshall of the Camp.

Duties: No real duties. Titles like Grand Falconer and Marshall of the Camp were ancient titles that had huge salaries but no real duties. The governor of Lille didn't govern but did get paid lots of rents.

Salaries: No-one really knows, but it would have been a fortune; millions of francs in modern money.

ELISABETH VIGÉE-LEBRUN

Probably deserved all the success she got – and some more. One of the greatest portrait painters of the 18th century. Her intimate, informal style of portrait painting – and her love of bold colours – perfectly matched the queen's taste for a simpler, more 'natural' style of clothes.

ROSE BERTIN

The queen's dressmaker, who made the loose white 'natural' looking dresses and hats the queen loved to wear. She became one of the most influential women in France, and made a fortune selling dresses to the queen, Princess la Lamballe, Gabrielle Yolande de Polignac and others.

Unfortunately, the queen's presents didn't stop just with her favourites themselves. Their uncles, aunts, friends and hangers-on got gifts and jobs too. The queen thought she was doing nothing wrong, just doing good turns to her friends. But that's not how the rest of the court saw it. Louis's brother the Count of Provence started calling her 'Madame Deficit' as if she was to blame for all the debts of France. It was a name and a reputation that stuck.

Chapter 6

Having a Baby – In Public

The event which stopped the gossip and scandal-making – at least for a while – was the long-awaited royal baby. In 1778, after eight years of marriage, the queen announced that she was pregnant for the first time (she would eventually have four children).

On 19th December 1778, the queen went into labour. As soon as it became obvious that the royal baby was about to be born, there was a mad scramble of courtiers to get into Marie Antoinette's bedroom to watch the birth.

It was an old tradition that any French citizen could watch a royal birth, so they could see for themselves that the baby really was the queen's and not a substitute. So in the room with the queen were her ladies-in-waiting, the king and his lords-in-waiting, Marie Antoinette's best friends the Princess de Lamballe and Gabrielle Yolande de Polignac, and the most important government ministers. Also present was anyone else who could push their way into the room. Several people stood on tables and chairs to get a better view.

BIRTH IN PROGRESS......

After an hour the queen gave birth to a daughter, which was delivered by the brother of her old tutor Vermond.

But there were so many people crammed into the room that the queen had a panic attack and couldn't breathe.

"Help me!" she groaned. "I'm dying!" and she fainted. Blood started trickling from her mouth and her nose.

One of the lords pushed his way to the window and tried to open it, but he couldn't. It was December, and the rule was that during the winter all the windows of Versailles were sealed with strips of wood which were nailed to the window frames to keep out the draughts. King Louis, who was extremely strong and fit, mainly due to his hunting, climbed onto the window seat, ripped off the wooden strips and flung open the window.

At first nothing happened. Many people thought that what the queen had said was true: she was going to die. Then slowly Marie Antoinette regained consciousness. As she did, the Princess de Lamballe, who didn't like to be left out of any dramas, fainted too and had to be carried out of the room.

Louis, not surprisingly, passed a law a little later which said that at future royal births the public would *not* be allowed to watch.

The old ways

Although life in the palace was happier for the king and queen now they had their baby, things were going badly wrong in the country Louis was supposed to be running.

Unlike Britain, France was ruled under the old, medieval feudal system. There were no elections in France and no parliament to make laws. The law was simply what the king said. He was an *absolute monarch* which meant that he had the absolute right to do whatever he liked. It also meant that when things went wrong, the king got the blame, whether it was his fault or not. And Louis was trapped, like everybody else, by the rigid system of French society.

Every French man or woman was a member of one of three classes or 'estates'. In some ways, France was like three different nations, each with its own laws.

The First Estate consisted of members of the clergy: priests, bishops, monks and nuns. The senior members of the clergy, the bishops and cardinals, were all from noble families. The senior clergy were therefore very rich.

The Second Estate was made up of the nobles, the lords and ladies who owned most of the land and were also the courtiers at Versailles. On their own lands they had similar powers to a king. They were also very rich. Most French farm workers were virtually slaves to the lords who owned the land on which they worked.

The Third Estate was everybody else, mostly the peasants who worked the land. Every year the peasants had to give part of their crops to their lord. They also had to work for no money building roads and bridges. French peasants had few possessions and virtually no money; the rich lords owned almost everything.

But it was the members of the Third Estate who paid the most taxes.

And not only did they pay taxes to the king, they also paid taxes to the church. All the senior churchmen, like the bishops and cardinals, came from the wealthiest families, and the rich clergy, like the nobles, paid virtually no taxes.

The system of government, like the system of rules at Versailles, was ridiculous. Everyone but a few nobles could see that change had to happen. The peasants were fed up with the unjust old ways, and so were the middle-class people living in the towns.

The middle classes wanted good jobs for themselves and their children. But all the best jobs – senior officers in the army, the top jobs in the church – were reserved by law for the nobles and their families.

Most French people wanted changes to the way France was ruled. They wanted new laws, an equal chance to get good jobs, a fair tax system. More than anything, they wanted an end to the privileges of the nobles; an end to their wasting of money on ridiculous clothes and expensive jewellery while ordinary people went hungry.

Chapter 7

Diamond Necklace Scandal

At exactly the worst possible moment, the queen became involved in a scandal which for many French people summed up everything they most hated about the old ways. And although she was the victim, the queen got the blame.

A Paris jeweller had made a diamond necklace for one of the old king, Louis XV's, girlfriends. It was enormous, the most expensive necklace ever made in France, and before he could pay for it the old king died.

The jeweller was desperate. He'd bought the diamonds, made the necklace and now no-one wanted it. If he didn't find

a buyer he would be ruined, possibly thrown into jail. He could think of only one person who could afford such a necklace: the queen.

He went to the palace, he tried flattery, he tried begging, he even tried throwing himself on the floor in front of the queen and sobbing his eyes out. It did no good, the queen simply didn't want the necklace. It was huge, it was ugly and it was much too expensive.

But two sharp crooks, a woman called Jeanne la Motte and her husband, heard about the necklace and saw a golden (or diamond) opportunity to make a fortune.

Jeanne la Motte went to one of the old courtiers at Versailles, Cardinal Rohan, and told the cardinal that the queen wanted to have the necklace desperately, but didn't want anyone to know. Would he buy it for her, in instalments, and the queen would pay him back? But he had to keep the deal absolutely secret.

Like a complete idiot, Rohan said "Yes". Anything to get in favour with the queen.

He went to the jeweller, promised the jeweller money and gave the necklace to Jeanne la Motte, who said she'd deliver it to the queen.

She didn't of course. She broke up the necklace and she and her husband sold the diamonds in France and Britain.

The truth finally came out when the jeweller went to Cardinal Rohan for his money, and Rohan then asked the queen.

There was a trial. The la Mottes and Rohan were put in jail, and... *everyone blamed Marie Antoinette.*

Le Télégraphe

AUSTRIAN QUEEN DOUBLE-DOUBLE CROSSES HONEST FRENCH COUPLE AND CARDINAL

Says she wants necklace then changes her mind ... when the bill arrives!

La Poste en Dimanche

QUEEN'S LIES JAIL FRENCH NOBLE AND FRIENDS

Madame Deficit adds to National Debt ... again!

LA SOLEIL

FOREIGN QUEEN TELLS PORKIES:

Does she want the necklace or doesn't she?

MADAME LA MOTTE BRANDED IN PUBLIC – PICTURES INSIDE!

Chapter 8

France in Crisis

But the diamond necklace affair was only a small matter compared to the awful mess Louis's government was in. France was bankrupt.

To pay for the Seven Years' War, the government of King Louis XV had borrowed lots of money. Because of the tax laws (with most of the taxes paid by the people who had the least money) it was impossible for the king to raise enough money to pay back the debts. Louis XVI had continued to borrow money. In 1789 the crunch came: no-one would lend him any more.

The only way out of the mess was to raise new taxes. Louis

knew that he couldn't tax the workers of the Third Estate any more, it simply wouldn't work. He had to tax the nobles.

But absolute monarch or not, Louis's new tax plan was stopped. The Paris law court, which was called the *parlement*, refused to allow the new law to be passed. They said the nobles couldn't be taxed, it was against all their privileges. Not surprisingly, the parlement was supported by the nobles and the clergy. With every day that passed without the new taxes France slid deeper and deeper into debt.

In desperation, the king called a meeting of the *Estates-General*, the ancient French Council (or parliament). He was sure they would support him.

The Estates-General met in Versailles. It was supposed to be three separate parliaments, one for each estate. But the representatives of the Third Estate wanted more than just the honour of saying "Yes, your majesty" to Louis's new tax plans. They could see that here was an opportunity to change not just the tax system, but the whole way France was governed.

The leaders of the Third Estate, backed by some nobles, demanded that the representatives of all three estates combine to form a proper parliament that could make new laws for France, just like the British parliament made laws for Britain. Reluctantly, Louis agreed.

The representatives called their new parliament the *National Assembly*. Unfortunately, the new National Assembly couldn't solve the immediate problem that was threatening France: hunger.

The Revolution starts

Most French people depended on bread as their main food. But in the summer of 1788, the year before the Estates General met, freak hailstorms had badly damaged the wheat and barley crops before they could be harvested. As if that wasn't bad enough, the winter had been the worst anyone could remember; rivers and lakes were frozen for months.

When the thaw came, the roads flooded. What little food had been saved from the hail and ice couldn't be got to the towns because of the flooded roads. The price of bread rocketed, and the poor people in cities like Paris began to starve.

For years the ordinary people – the workers in the towns as well as the peasants in the countryside – had been angry about the large amount of taxes they had to pay compared to the tiny amounts paid by the rich nobles, and how the nobles showed off their wealth by building huge houses, wearing expensive clothes and driving around in enormous carriages. The shortage of food was the final straw.

When the lack of food spread to Paris in the early summer of 1789, the poor people of Paris took to the streets in increasingly violent demonstrations. They wanted change – now. They couldn't afford to wait for Louis and the National Assembly to make new laws. By the time new laws were passed they could be dead from starvation.

The demonstrators summed up what they wanted in a slogan which they chanted as they marched: *Liberté! Egalité! Fraternité!* (Freedom! Equality! Brotherhood!) …and they wanted it now.

Louis and the new National Assembly realized that they had lost control. An angry mob of working people had taken to the streets, demanding food and freedom. They were nicknamed the *sans-culottes*, because they didn't wear knee-length breeches (culottes) like the nobles, but wore rough, ankle-length trousers. The sans-culottes had shown by their violent demonstrations that they were prepared to kill anyone who got in their way. A violent revolution had begun.

What do we want?...FooD! when do we want it?...Now!

In October 1789, a crowd of women demanding bread, marched from Paris to the royal palace at Versailles. They shouted for the king to give them food, and they also sang songs about Marie Antoinette; how much they hated her, and how she was to blame for the troubles of France.

The mob of women smashed their way into the palace. They killed two of the king's bodyguards and threatened to kill the queen as well – unless the royal family came with them to live in the Tuileries Palace in Paris immediately.

The king, desperate to protect the queen and his children, agreed. The royal family got into a coach and a procession set off to travel the 14 kilometres to Paris. At the head of the procession were two men carrying sharpened poles. On top of the poles were the heads of the guards who had been killed.

Chapter 9

Escape!

Horrified at what was happening in Paris, and fearing for the safety of the queen and his children, Louis planned an escape for the family.

The plan was for the family to travel northeast from Paris by coach to a town called Montmédy near the border with the Austrian Netherlands (nowadays Belgium). At Montmédy there were troops that were still loyal to the king. There the royal family would be safe.

Coaches, changes of horses and an escort of soldiers were all arranged. The escape was set for 20th June 1791, nearly two years after the start of the Revolution.

1. 20ᵗʰ June, 10:00 pm: Royal family put on disguises – Louis dresses as a servant, dauphin dressed as a girl. Louis and children get to coach on time.

2. Marie-Antoinette is almost caught trying to leave, gets lost in palace corridors for 30 minutes.

3. 12 midnight: Coach doesn't leave Paris straight away but drives to safe house where everyone waits for two hours while the coachman checks arrangements for next change of horses.

4. Reaches place where change of coaches is to take place. So dark that at first no-one can find new coach. More delay.

5. New coach so big and slow it can only travel at 7 kph.

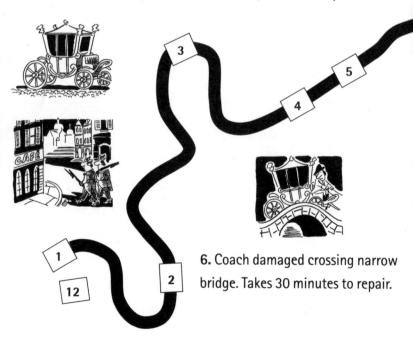

6. Coach damaged crossing narrow bridge. Takes 30 minutes to repair.

7. Escort of soldiers should be waiting at Pont de Somme-Vesle. Because coach two hours 30 minutes late, soldiers have gone.

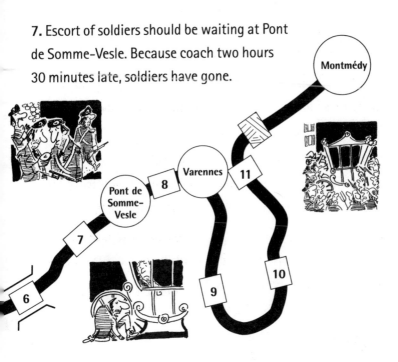

Montmédy

Varennes

11

Pont de Somme-Vesle

8

7

6

9

10

8. June 21st 11.00 pm: Reach Varennes. Should be a change of horses. No horses.

9. Coach stopped by villagers. A villager who used to work at Versailles recognises the king.

10. Royal family spend night at house of local magistrate.

11. June 22nd 6.00 am: Try to continue journey, but stopped at barricade on bridge. Surrounded by 6,000 armed men. Royal family captured and...

12. June 25th: Royal family back at Tuileries Palace, Paris.

13. If only...

War against Austria

In March 1792, Marie Antoinette's brother Leopold, the Austrian emperor, died. The new emperor, Francis II, Marie Antoinette's nephew, was determined to destroy the French Revolution and rescue his aunt. He and the King of Prussia publicly promised to help Louis and Marie Antoinette. They also called on the other kings of Europe to join them.

The French army attacked first, but the Austrian and Prussian armies were much better organised and equipped. There were rumours, probably true, that Marie Antoinette was sending the secret battle plans of the French army to her nephew, who shared them with the Prussians.

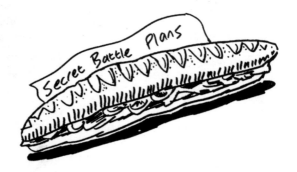

The National Assembly gave weapons to all the citizens of Paris so that they could defend themselves. What they did instead was to use their new weapons to attack the prisons and massacre all the prisoners (the aristocrats) they could find.

The Prussian army came within a few miles of Paris before being beaten by the French army.

The Paris mob, which was now well armed, turned on the king and royal family. They believed the king and queen were to blame for the danger France was in: they were traitors and should be punished.

Helped by the National Guard, the mob attacked the Tuileries Palace and killed the king's bodyguard of 600 Swiss Guards. The royal family fled to the Assembly building and asked the members for protection.

The Assembly decided to send the royal family – which consisted of Louis's sister Elisabeth, Louis, Marie Antoinette and their two surviving children, the dauphin Louis-Charles and his sister Marie-Thérèse – to the Temple Prison. Only Marie-Thérèse would survive their imprisonment.

The Reign of Terror

Another group emerged to take control of the Revolution. They were called *Jacobins*. They weren't working people like the sans-culottes – the poor people of Paris who made up the mob

– but middle-class revolutionaries. They were led by a young lawyer called Maximilien Robespierre.

The sans-culottes had had enough of politicians and kings; enough of plots and treason. They decided it was time for action, and time to get rid of the old ways for good.

There was only one way to get rid of the old ways for good, according to the radicals of the Jacobins and the leaders of the sans-cullottes, and that was to kill every aristocrat and everyone who might be an enemy of the Revolution.

A committee was set up in Paris controlled by Robespierre and a man named Danton, who was the leader of the sans-culottes. It was called the Committee of Public Safety and decided who was or was not an enemy of the Revolution. It put the whole of France under military law. This is part of the actual decree that the Committee issued:

Liberty, Equality or Death

...the young men shall go to battle; the married men shall forge arms and transport supplies; women shall make tents and serve in hospitals; the children shall tear bandages; and old men shall go to public squares and preach the unity of the Republic and hatred of kings.

For anyone found guilty of not supporting the new republic there was only one punishment: death. In a single year, between 1793 and 1794, on the orders of the Committee, nearly 18,000 people were executed in France. In Paris alone, more than 3,000 were executed. It was known as the *Reign of Terror.*

All the executions were carried out in public, in front of large crowds which often booed and threw rotting rubbish at the condemned prisoners as they were driven to the scaffold on open carts called tumbrils.

Chapter 10

Madame Guillotine

It would have been impossible to execute so many people if it hadn't been for a new, mechanized means of killing people: the guillotine.

Under the old feudal laws, only criminals who came from the noble families were allowed to be beheaded. Most other criminals were hanged. Believe it or not, it was thought to be a privilege to be beheaded.

The revolutionaries believed in equality. They decided that everyone who was condemned to death should have the same privileges as the aristocrats. If beheading was good enough for the nobility, then it was good enough for everyone.

There was one problem, though: cutting someone's head off isn't as easy as you might think. It takes a lot of skill to do it properly, and it can be hard work. An executioner couldn't behead more than a few people a day before he got too tired to work properly.

In 1789, a member of the National Assembly, a doctor called Joseph-Ignace Guillotin, came up with a solution. He told the Assembly that he'd been working to improve a mechanical beheading machine which had been used, but not very successfully, in the past. It would, he assured the Assembly, be a quick and humane way of killing large numbers of people.

The idea wasn't taken up until early 1792, when another doctor, this time called Louis, suggested the same plan to the Assembly. Dr Louis employed a German piano maker to build a prototype. Then he tested it on dead bodies from the hospital at Bicêtre, and it worked very well.

The first machine was set up in the Place Grève in Paris for the execution of a highwayman on 25th April, 1792. At first the machine was called Louisette, or Louison, after Dr Louis. But it soon got the nickname *la guillotine*, or *madame guillotine*

after Dr Guillotin, the man who had first suggested using it for public executions.

The King must die

One of the first victims of the Reign of Terror was the king himself.

In August 1792, the Assembly declared France a republic, a state without a monarch. Instead of being called Louis XVI, the Assembly said that he was now to be called Citizen Capet.

CITIZEN CAPET

The King of France had always been seen as a special person: for example, his coronation was called the *sacre* (like sacred). But now the king was no longer special; he was no longer above the law.

On 11th December 1792 the king was charged with treason.

His trial began in January, 1793.

Just as King Charles I of England had been tried for treason by the English Parliament in 1649, Louis was to be tried by the French equivalent – which now called itself the *National Convention*.

There were many charges against Louis, including:

 Ordering his troops to shoot demonstrators.

 Trying to raise a secret army to put down the Revolution.

 Making a fortune buying and selling coffee and sugar.

 Giving money to the poor to make himself more popular.

Louis's lawyers did their best, but the Jacobins and sans-culottes would settle for nothing less than a guilty verdict and the death sentence. On 16th January 1793, after 37 hours of voting by the deputies in the National Convention, they got what they wanted.

Louis hadn't been allowed to see his family for six weeks, but he was now allowed to spend his last evening with them. Typically, he seems to have spent the evening trying to comfort them rather than feeling sorry for himself.

He told his young son Louis-Charles, who would become king the next day, not to try to avenge his death. He told Louis-Charles and his daughter, Marie-Thérèse, always to be obedient to their mother.

At ten o'clock, he went back to his room.

Louis's valet, Cléry, who had been allowed to stay with the king in prison to look after him, woke him at five o'clock the following morning. Louis then took Communion from an English priest, Father Edgeworth. He gave his wedding ring to Cléry and asked him to give it to the queen. He also gave Cléry a seal from his watch-chain to give to his son the dauphin as a sign that he was now King Louis XVII.

Later, Cléry wrote in his diary:

I remained alone in the room, numb with grief. The drums and the trumpets announced that His Majesty left the prison. An hour later, salvoes of artillery and cries of Long Live The Nation! and Long Live The Republic! filled the air. The best of kings was no more!

Louis was driven in a closed coach from the Temple Prison to the Place de la Révolution where the guillotine had been put up. When he reached the main platform, Louis tried to make a speech:

I die innocent of all the crimes of which I have been charged. I pardon those who have brought about my death and I pray that the blood you are about to shed may never be required of France...

At that point, the officer in charge ordered the drum-roll to start, and the rest of the king's speech was drowned out. The king was strapped to the plank of the guillotine, lowered into position and the blade fell.

The executioner lifted the severed head of the king out of the basket and held it up to show the crowd that Louis XVI was dead.

Chapter 11

Marie Antoinette
on Trial

Now that the king was dead, the Committee of Public Safety
turned on the queen. They started a campaign of mental
torture against her, to break her will before the trial they were
planning began.

First, Louis-Charles, her sickly seven-year-old son, was taken
away from her. He was taken to a cell below Marie
Antoinette's and handed over to a vicious shoemaker called
Simon who used to hit and humiliate the boy. Often, Marie
Antoinette could hear her son sobbing for hours on end.

Then, just before her trial was due to begin, Marie Antoinette was separated from the last two members of her family, her daughter Marie-Thérèse and her sister-in-law Elisabeth. She was taken from the Temple Prison to the Conciergerie Prison, where she was kept in a tiny cell. There were two guards with her night and day, but they weren't allowed to speak to her.

Marie Antoinette's trial was even more of a fixed show trial than Louis's had been.

At a secret session of the Committee of Public Safety, Jacques Hébert, one of Marie Antoinette's most bitter enemies and editor of the newspaper *Père Duchesne* had demanded Marie Antoinette be put on trial. He said:

I have promised my readers Marie Antoinette's head. If there is any delay in giving it to me, I shall go and cut it off myself… The mob will kill all our enemies, but their zeal must be kept on the boil, and you can only do that by putting Marie Antoinette to death.

Marie Antoinette's trial took three days. All the rumours which had been spread by the court about Marie Antoinette's behaviour were brought up at the trial. For days before the trial began, newspapers like Hébert's *Père Duchesne* had been calling the queen things like:

The Austrian she-wolf …the arch tigress… a monster who needed to slake her thirst on the blood of the French …who wanted to roast all the poor Parisians alive.

Louis had more or less accepted that he was doomed, but Marie Antoinette answered every accusation, fought against every lie the prosecution told. But it did no good. The hatred which the people felt for her – stirred up by papers like *Père Duchesne* – made the result certain. She was condemned to death.

Nowadays, famous people who are tried for a serious offence often give interviews to the newspapers or TV. In

America, convicted criminals on Death Row give interviews from prison.

Marie Antoinette couldn't give this sort of interview once she was sentenced. But this is what she might have said, if she had:

MARIE ANTOINETTE: The interview that never was

Q What's your favourite place?

A The Petit Trianon, where I can be a normal person, away from the prying eyes of jealous, gossiping courtiers with their ridiculous rules and etiquette.

Q What was your favourite recreational activity?

A Acting in plays at the little theatre there, and going to the theatre and opera in Paris with friends.

Q Who were your best friends?

A The Princess la Lamballe and Gabrielle Yolande de Polignac.

Q What was your favourite picture of yourself?

A A portrait by Elisabeth Vigée-Lebrun in which I am wearing a simple, Creole-style dress, with a wide-brimmed hat with a feather. I'm making a posy of roses.

Q What was your least favourite?

A A picture of myself and the children in front of an empty cradle. I'd just lost a baby, and Louis Joseph, who was then dauphin, was already ill. It reminds me of my poor dead children and makes me very sad.

Q Why was such a depressing picture painted?

A I was told it would make people see the real me, the person behind all the rumours and lies that were being spread. I was told it would make the ordinary people feel sorry for a grieving mother and make me popular again.

Q Did it work?

A No.

Q Were you ever popular?

A Oh, yes! When I first came to Paris to marry the king thousands of people came to cheer. And one of the ministers said to me: "Madame, 20,000 people have fallen in love with you." Bah!

Q What do you blame for your unpopularity?

A Jealousy and racism. The courtiers were jealous, and the people hated me just because they thought I was Austrian.

Q But you were Austrian, weren't you?

A Not really. My father was French, the Duke of Lorraine. I was brought up as a child to speak French. I was a French citizen for 23 years. What more could I do? In any case, my husband Louis's mother was German, so you could say he was as French – or as un-French – as me.

Q What's your favourite word?

A Friendship.

Q Who was the love of your life?

A My children.

Q Not your husband, Louis?

A The King and I were married to make a treaty. I was never in love with him, and he was never in love with me. We ended up having the most enormous liking and respect for each other. He was a wonderful father, and a dignified and brave man. But no, I never loved him as a lover.

Q Did you ever love anyone else – as a lover?

A None of your business.

Q What qualities do you most dislike in other people?

A Jealousy and making scandals.

Q What quality would you most like to change in yourself?

A Perhaps I was too generous to my friends. It made me unpopular, and made them unpopular too.

Q What qualities do you think others most admire in you?

A Courage and determination, in not giving up trying to be a good queen when everyone turned against me. Remaining brave when I was falsely accused of crimes I didn't commit.

Q What do you most regret?

A Not escaping earlier in the Revolution when we had the chance.

Chapter 12

The End

Marie Antoinette was taken back to the Concièrgerie. In her cell, she wrote a last letter to Elisabeth, her sister-in-law, asking her to look after Louis-Charles and Marie-Thérèse. Then she changed into a plain white dress, white bonnet and a pair of plum-coloured high-heeled shoes.

She was horrified to see an open tumbril arrive to take her to the guillotine. She'd been expecting the privacy of a closed carriage like Louis had. Bravely, she sat upright and unflinching in the cart. Many of the people in the crowds didn't recognize her. Her reddish blonde hair had turned completely white during her imprisonment.

She was still only 37 years old when she died, but people who saw her that day said she could have passed for 50 or even 60.

What happened to...

LOUIS-CHARLES (the dauphin): When his father died, he became – in the eyes of the royalists – King Louis XVII. He was only eight years old when his mother was executed. Simon, his jailer, was guillotined during the Terror. After that, Louis-Charles was kept in solitary confinement. No one talked to him and his food was passed to him through a little opening at the bottom of his cell door. He lived in dreadful conditions. There are stories that he was rescued from the prison, but unfortunately they aren't true. He died in June 1795 in the Temple Prison of the 'family disease': TB.

MARIE-THERESE: Survived the Reign of Terror and imprisonment. In December 1795 she was allowed to leave France as part of an exchange of prisoners captured during the war against Austria and Prussia. She eventually married her cousin, the eldest son of the Duke of Artois, and returned to the Tuileries as a princess after the restoration of the monarchy in 1814.

ELISABETH (sister of Louis XVI): Remained in the Temple Prison until it was her turn to face the guillotine. During her last few weeks in prison she passed the time by embroidering a picture of a skull. Underneath were the words: 'This is my only thought'.

PRINCESS LA LAMBALLE: Was imprisoned. In September 1792 she refused to swear an oath saying that she hated the king and queen. To punish her for this, the prison guards threw her out of the prison to the mob waiting outside who killed her.

GABRIELLE YOLANDE DE POLIGNAC: Escaped from France, but in 1793 she caught a mystery illness and died within 12 hours.

ELISABETH VIGEE-LEBRUN: Left France when the Revolution started. She spent the next 12 years travelling through Europe, painting portraits. She lived in London and Switzerland, finally returning to Paris in 1810.

She wrote a book of memoirs which was published in 1837. She died in Paris at the age of 86. During her career she painted 622 portraits and 200 landscapes.

DUKE OF PROVENCE: Escaped from France in 1791 and organized groups to overthrow the Revolution, which didn't help his brother and sister-in-law. In 1795, when the dauphin died, Provence declared himself to be King Louis XVIII. He came back to France as king in 1814, though with a parliament to vote on laws. He reigned until his death in 1824.

DUKE OF ARTOIS: Was ordered to leave France in 1789 by Louis. After travelling around Europe he returned to France in 1814 when his brother became king. Artois became a politician, leading a party of ultra-royalists who wanted France to get rid of every trace of the Revolution and return to the old style of absolute monarchy. When his brother died in 1824, he became King Charles X. He and his government were very unpopular, and in 1830 he was forced to give up the throne when there was, once again, a revolution in Paris. He died in Prague six years later.

ROBESPIERRE: The Reign of Terror, organised by Robespierre, continued until 1794. Having executed all the aristocrats and other 'enemies of the Revolution' the Revolutionary Tribunals, encouraged by Robespierre, began trying and executing politicians.

Eventually, the other members of the Committee of Public Safety turned on Robespierre. He was arrested, tried and guillotined in August 1794.

THE REVOLUTION: After Robespierre's death, France was ruled by five directors. The government became more and more corrupt and inefficient. Eventually, an army officer called Napoleon Bonaparte organised a coup – he threw out the government by force. He became military dictator of France, and then declared himself emperor.

After many years of war against Austria, Russia, Prussia and Britain, Napoleon's army was eventually defeated at the battle of Waterloo in 1815.

There are a few beans I could spill about Napoleon... but that is another story.

titles in the series